LOOK TO THE CROCUS

PREVIOUS BOOKS BY MARION McCREADY

Tree Language, Eyewear Publishing, 2014
Madame Ecosse, Eyewear Publishing, 2017

Printed by imprintdigital
Upton Pyne, Exeter
www.digital.imprint.co.uk

Typesetting and cover design by The Book Typesetters
hello@thebooktypesetters.com
07422 598 168
www.thebooktypesetters.com

Published by Shoestring Press
19 Devonshire Avenue, Beeston, Nottingham, NG9 1BS
(0115) 925 1827
www.shoestringpress.co.uk

First published 2023
© Copyright: Marion McCready
© Cover image: Brigid Collins

ISBN 978-1-915553-26-3

LOOK TO THE CROCUS

MARION McCREADY

Shoestring Press

ACKNOWLEDGEMENTS

My ballad poems were inspired by the Child Ballads which are a collection of traditional ballads from Scotland and England gathered and anthologised in the nineteenth century by Francis James Child.

My thanks to the editors of the following publications where some of these poems, or versions of them, first appeared: *Poetry (Chicago), Poetry Ireland Review, The Manchester Review, Poetry Salzburg Review, Northwords Now, Poetry Scotland, The Glasgow Herald, Stand, The Manhattan Review, Marble Poetry Magazine, Dreich*; and online *at Poetry Daily, London Grip, Atrium, Ink, Sweat & Tears,* and *The Ofi Press* (Mexico). Some of these poems also appeared in the following anthologies: *Greek Anthology of Young Scottish Poets* (Vakxikon Publications), *Beyond the Swelkie: Celebration of George Mackay* Brown (Tippermuir Books); *Summer Anywhere* (Dreich). 'The Telephone Box' was commended in the Cheltenham Buzzwords competition (2020).

A big thank you to Brigid Collins for creating the cover image for this book. I am particularly grateful to John Killick for his encouragement and enthusiastic support for my work, for his insightful editorial reading and for being so central to bringing this collection to publication. My heartfelt thanks also to John Lucas for his close reading, editorial support and Shoestring Press for making this book possible.

In memory of my parents

In the depth of winter, I finally learned that within me
there lay an invincible summer

Albert Camus

CONTENTS

Flowers & Trees

Deep in their roots, all flowers keep the light

Theodore Roethke

LOOK TO THE CROCUS

Eyelids are the final petals closing on this life.
When I die, place crocuses on my eyes – they will guide me.

I kneel down next to the crocuses, touch them gingerly as if
        they were puppies
with pin teeth jumping excitedly in the firth breeze.

At last the snow has left us, cleaned the earth for crocuses
luxurious as silky hair or oiled skin.

Don't be fooled – crocuses are wild as a fairground wheel
spinning out of control. The crocuses were coughed up out of
        the ground;

they are scattered round tree trunks like residue from a terrible
        accident.
They are purple tears hand-sewn to the earth.

We are all survivors in this life, but none more so than the crocus
embedded in the grass like a microchip gathering the history of
        the world.

Crocuses are purple submarines moving silently though green
        waves.
The crocuses seem to be melting among snowdrops like ice-cream

with the wet look of a frog; their orange tongue-pistils barely
        visible.
Crocuses are satellites in the grass watching us, they know us

better than we know ourselves. Look to the crocus.
Do not stand on the purple crocus, it will remember your
        footprint.

The crocus beckons like homemade liqueur –
each one a glassful of sunlight. The crocus is a soft word in my ear;

the crocus is my best self. I carry it around in my head like a song.
I want to crawl inside its purple armour – dwell in the honeyed
      saffron

filaments at its centre. Thank God when the final curtain falls
it is made of crocuses.

BLEEDING HEARTS

Bleeding hearts roam through the garden
on arched stems, drawing into them
the slow pilgrims of spring – butterflies
(painted lady, brimstone, holy blue).

And what will they find there?
An open room, a theatre of light.

Bleeding hearts in the garden hang
in a row, their pendulums swinging,
keeping time, divining answers –
      yes and no.

Tiny hot air balloons,
they glow, fired-up and sailing
through the sky. Delivering messages
from somewhere beyond the ear,
      beyond the eye.

The sun has made its home
in the burst fruit of the flushed bloom.

Bleeding hearts in the garden voyage
in bubbles of light like blown glass
      formed in a crucible.

Listen, hear their sound bath
like the bells of St. Clement's
ringing through the air,

rising in the heart – the rhymes
of a child to be summoned to mind
      anytime, anywhere.

ROWAN

You planted a rowan by the front door to watch over me.
Between leaves, the blue sky creates symbols –
a radioactive trefoil, a lightning bolt, downward flying dove.

I have lived all my life under the gaze of the rowan.
I follow rowan trees to find my way home.
At night, tart berries float through a black sky
like a choir of red women.

This tree in my garden is a bird catcher;
it is my *ran,* my *roan,* my *rodan,* my *royan,* my *royne,*
my *rune,* my *mountain ash,* my *quicken-tree,*
my *wicken-tree* for the waxwings and the thrush.

In a dream the rowan took off from my garden,
flew over the house like a heron.
In the morning I hear the call of the rowan;
its heavy load warns of a difficult winter.

THE BRANCHES OF MY HEART ARE STEEL WIRE

In the split Y of its trunk the winter birch
sucks and holds the life of the garden.

I am a dowsing rod – I follow pulses, sonar,
Morse, vibrations drumming through air

and hold them in the atrium, courtyard,
sunken pools of my heart.

Winter birch in fog, branches like steel wire,
tiny spiders scuttling across the sky.

I watch, wait for you to come close.
Your footsteps tread through blunt grass.

All night, I too am birch. I inhabit the garden
in my sleeping body. In daytime

it appears, stigmata, in the veins
in my wrists, on the backs of my hands.

Winter birch scraping against a frog moon.
Your branches, a fish net, slowly lowers

around me. If I could climb your prongs,
I would summon this amphibian satellite

into my arms by the tides of my grey eyes,
to light up every limb and sinew of body and birch.

THE BRAHAN SEER'S WIFE

Prologue

Tulips contain cities inside the sunset
of their open skies. What worlds live within,
whose lives? Though my husband has seen it all –
our days are governed by a stone with a hole

waiting for its call (visions of black rain / blood
on Drumossie moor / sheep eating the men),
he thinks of nothing else. Though he has seen it all,
my husband is blind to the life of a tulip.

I

When he bought me tulips, I knew they were a sign.
Twenty-two yellow tulips in a stoneware jug.
Twenty-two mummified pharaohs rolling
through the streets of Cairo in nitrogen capsules –
eighteen kings, four queens.
                              Nightly, I count
closed sockets of twenty-two yellow tulips,
yellow Cambrian pincers rising top-heavy
from the green wands of their stalks.

Eyeless arthropods, they dream of sun. The pharaohs
travel by night unharmed by the soft gel of dusk
soothing their journey.
                        I, too, travel by night
like the tawny owl hunting outside my bedroom window.
Though he won't say, I know he's seen my end
prophesied through the eye of an adder stone.

I know the signs – curse of the mummy,
mottled owl swooping toward us all.

His silence is unbearable.
Perhaps that's why I dream of flying
like an arrow into the bullseye of a tulip.

II

When tulips rise out of the brown stoneware jug
that belonged to my late mother-in-law,
        their yellowness draws me in.
I look for a warm pool at the bottom of the tulips
to step into, a yellow bath to emerge from.

I imagine tulips growing from my fingertips,
great bulbs of the sky in motion as I raise my hands
through the air. They multiply in the mirror.
        Tulips in the mirror are a gift.
From the other side of the glass, they are given.

III

When he brought me rainbow tulips,
        they orbited the room.
Inside each one is a solar system
spiralling downward.

Tulips are wormholes, they open for me,
they draw me in. I swim in their red depths,
their fathomless purple.
                My tulips transmit,
they receive messages from the night.
Their antennae point to somewhere beyond

9

this bedroom ceiling, beyond the slate roof
up to a black April sky.

The tips of the flowers are singed
as if held out to a small flame;
like a token offering to some god or other.

They carry the tart beauty of a sunset,
badge pin piercing skin drawing blood,
prophesying, long before my husband –
        red sky at night...

IV

It's the final flourish,
my tulips have succumbed to their end,

petals folding in on themselves
like arthritic fingers.

They do not die but come into their own –
creatures of Sultans,

their skin rippling, bees sleeping
in their mouths.

My tulips decompose
into an earthy symphony

and I am the conductor
through which their music flows.

"THE COMPLICATED SEX LIFE OF PRIMULA...
fascinated Charles Darwin"
(Science Daily)

A Mardi Gras of primroses line my driveway.
Pin-eyed, thrum-eyed, natural selection in action;

the carnival of primroses grow in number daily.
Every spring they perform street theatre, they perform

the Easter story with beads, feathers and leather tongues.
Yellow vests, they agitate against the March snow; late

calling cards of winter. They are frozen cells of embryos
waiting to live. In my garden, cultivated,

I have red primroses; I have blue. Posy-globes in orbit,
they contain unconquered territories. Spring after spring

primroses unveil their watchful eyes, opening
despite the northeasterlies. When thaw comes, I paint

my body half-primrose, hang a nosegay of thirteen primroses
by my front door. I look into a primrose the way one

looks into a mirror to see the same exaggerated grin;
the same teardrop staining the face.

POINSETTIA

It sits on a gilt plate, photo still of fireworks shooting off
in all directions, red tips of leaves coming together

in a delicate point like an onion dome.
Poinsettia, once you were a gift from my mother

then you became a remembrance of her.
Now you are a bird of fire moving through air.

Your leaves burn a hole in my table which cannot be filled.
I smell your soil, black grains, pot of earth.

Your soil fills my veins, feeding the poinsettia unfurling in my
        chest;
the heart that has now shrunk to a tight fist.

Poinsettia flies its red flag and marches across my oak table.
Poinsettia is a swarm of butterflies. A strawberry field

which seemed so far off has now travelled toward me
lighting a sunset on my skin; ruby shade under my chin.

The poinsettia is ascending; a Jacob's ladder of leaves.
I climb the ladder of my thoughts reaching up to the red sky

stretching away from me; its red hope paling into the distance.

WINTER HYDRANGEA

Winter hydrangea growing through a screen of blunt light.
Teal and magenta mouths like a packed nest of hatchlings,
blind and impatient. Colouring grey air, climbing rungs
of the sky and unsinkable machines of clouds.
What do your bright colours mean in midwinter?
Are they traffic lights, signalling stop! And go!?
There is mathematics in your petals, order flows
up from the ground through to your panicles.
Do you rotate at night following planetary bodies
slow elephant lumber across the dark language of space?
Hydrangea. Flower heads larger than houses.
Like wet silk or blown glass, your drowsy top-heavy
blooms seem to levitate, a magician's assistant floating
above the stage, floating and opening; untouchable spheres.

STUDY OF DYING FLOWERS

The crystal vase, clouded,
drained of nutrient water weeks ago
has become a funerary urn
for a bouquet of Christmas flowers.

Stuck to the inside of the vase –
a large green leaf
marred with dark patches
like maria seas of the moon.

White daises, *day's eyes,*
rays have closed on themselves
hiding the central disk-face of the flower
which has aged from golden saffron

to ground cinnamon; ray florets
stained like used teabags.
The hung head of a deep wine daisy
is a dying swan – holding its death

mid-air. An unknown purple flower
is parched and rusted; it has been
through the fires. Some of its petals
have already departed.

But the centre of the unknown flower
is warm honey – an unexpected sunset
singing in the corner of my kitchen.
The kind of singing that rises with wings

from the bedside of a loved one
lifting them up and carrying them through
the great swing doors of the afterlife.

NARCISSI

When March snow fell, the monkey puzzle tree
rejoiced in the neighbour's garden.

Invisible bushes, ignored
like the homeless in Buchanan Street,
filled out suddenly, became three-dimensional animals
supplicating on either side of the road.

Like a jellyfish bell, the satellite dish hovered
above a long-empty house.
When snow fell, narcissi in the garden
bore the weight of fallen clouds.
I saved five for my crystal blue vase.

I picked five narcissi, explored their petals
with my lips. The petals overlap
in a circle of hands, each one lying
across another. Five narcissi in a crystal blue vase
became five hearts beating simultaneously.

Next day, the snow melted. The unexpected safari
became an ordinary street again.
But the narcissi in the window burn brighter;
orange and yellow hot air balloons.
They carry me out of this winter.

I DID NOT KNOW YOU, MONIACK MHOR

but you have always been there
in one guise or another.
I trace the range of Strathfarrar
    with my finger,
I draw the line of it in the air.

There is no sea, no sea here,
no *Juno*, *Jupiter* or *Saturn*
(ships of my childhood).

At Moniack Mhor I lie with the bees,
their still bodies floating above me.
A horse rider clips in the lower valley,
    curlews cry at my ear.

Hills fall behind hills,
behind hills. Moniack Mhor
is forever opening –
a gift of dry grass, crab clouds,
green nest of furze slowly breaking apart.

Nightly the yellow almond buds
    creep closer,
until I can taste them in the dark air.

THE ORANGE TREES OF ALTEA

A row of orange trees, five of them, five gifts
unwrapped and standing like a guard of watchmen.
The orange trees unburden their scent
as I walk under them. They welcome me
at regular intervals. Wrinkled and overripe,
oranges are veterans of the night.
The wind rolls in from the Mediterranean.
The oranges do not live in glass bowls
on Welsh dressers – heirlooms from the dead –
but instead float through a sky of Spanish blue;
blue distilled into a topaz on my finger.
The orange trees are a dream of five treasure chests.
I want to lift them out of the ground, cup
the orange heart of them close to me.

The orange trees of Altea rain their blossoms
down on me. On a hot night, the Mediterranean
floats over steep hills and rests on me. This beach,
on this Costa Blanca coast, bears soft pebbles
slipping down to the sea, caught in a white wrath
of waves. I finger two pebbles in my pocket,
perfectly round, warm stones and there is nothing left
but the sea, dark sky, the ice mountains of Sierra Helada
and me. And a dream of five orange trees.

I FALL IN LOVE WITH A TREE EVERYWHERE I GO

When I shut my eyes all I see is the sky hung with oranges
like a dozen orange golf balls;
the tree itself on display like a circus animal.

I am where palm trees rise and fall on the horizon;
where the scent of orange trees gathers pace in the air;
where my skin, my hair take on the spirit of citrus.

I pluck an orange tree blossom and it parts in my hand,
each petal pushing its scent through me like the strong
perfume
of the women of my childhood.

The belly of the orange tree is a play of light and shade.
Leaves flicker like cats' eyes.
Oranges move imperceptibly dark then bright,

dark then bright. I stand beneath the tree so long
oranges have become part of the sky
and the tree itself conducts me into another world.

APPLE OF MY TREE

If nothing else it was a good year for apples
at Auchamore Road.
Apples multiplied daily like protesters
outside a corrupt parliament.

The apples are now ready, an invisible jay
is singing to them. His voice, the sound
of planets moving in space.

*

Share an apple with me –
you have the green half, I'll have the red.
Let our lips meet in the middle.

The apples have come from my own garden.
I watched them grow and then with a twist
freed them from the arm of the tree.

They glow in a bowl in my kitchen,
silky skinned, they appeared suddenly.
A song of apples – each one holds its own note,
has its own key.

The bowl brings them together, a garden harmony.
The apples have brought garden life into my kitchen –
sounds of the rowan, jackdaw, pigeon.

When I bite into one, your lips meet mine.
Your eyes, dark seeds.
When I eat an apple I taste your lips –
earthy and sweet.

I've taken to wearing silver hearts
and dreaming of silver apples.

In my dream I gather them, hold them
in my hands. They have grown for me,
the garden gifts them to me.
When I peel an apple, its skin falls in letters
at my feet and it speaks to me –

apple of my tree.

WHEN I WASN'T LOOKING, THE GARDEN WREN

came to me, drawn to the wilds
of my long ferns and grasses.
When I wasn't looking, a song
of three trees came to me through the frame
of a train window. The wren,

with his brown eyes, stared into me.
I close my eyes and lean against a tree,
feel its solid bark mould to me.

I lean against a tree and swallow the star
lodged in its branches.

I dream my way back to the three beech trees
that came to me through a train window.

I snap a forked twig and carve my name into it.
Wrap ribbons and beads round it.

To be fed by the wren,
to become bird and star, emit sparks
like train tracks in the heat of the day…

The field stretches out into mist
in waves of yellow and green.

What do the birds, the trees say?
The sky is simply cut out around them.

FUCHSIAS ARE FALLING, IT IS MID-JULY –

I wrote that line three months ago.
Now it is mid-October and beech leaves are halos
of bronze through which I look at the grey sky –
miniature lights floating above my head.

The beech leaves look at me knowing their end.
They are drinking the last rays of autumn light,
their drunken bodies now crumpling to the ground.
When they fall it's as if strands of hair

are being pulled from my head. I am generous,
I leave long blonde tokens – sewing threads –
everywhere I go, sewing my words
onto anything that will take them.

My pockets are bloated with beech charms –
they speak to me from the end
of a crackling phone line
and from somewhere deep inside, I answer.

ON ANOTHER DAY

January branches are growing fingers and thumbs –
a mass of black shoots, twigs crocheting
across the lower vista.

The branches above us are embossed
with woodcut silhouettes – magpies
and collared doves.

What is love but the tenderness
of these small animals; their soft bodies
at rest. At twilight, the sky

is smoky purple and leaking
small clouds; a knocked-over lava lamp
dripping across the horizon.

Winter's chilled hooves chase us back inside
as the shutters of night slide down,
bolting the door on another day of our lives.

PINK RHODODENDRONS

They are opening toward me
like a gang of babies, or puppies,
or wedding bouquets;
    creatures from another world.

The porous coral sponges
    float through air
surprising as a flow of blood-clouds
from an underwater cut –

ballooning, changing, an ever-circling
    smoke trail.
The ones nearest enclose me
in their pink gowns of crepe and silk.

They grow in the mind's eye,
stamens stretching.
    I draw them into me,
they blossom in me and I in them.

The rhododendrons fill me.
    When they fall,
they lose pieces of themselves;
I lose myself also.

Each flower is a funicular
into another life, another time
    all here and now,
together, reverberating.

SHE SITS AMONG GINKGO AND DOG ROSE
for Brigid Collins

In the Physic Garden the split fins of the ginkgo leaves
    fan the air, their parts radiating
        like a stream of yellow fish –

they swim toward her in shoals, turning, twisting.
    In synchrony, they sweep past her.
        Past the sketch book

where the sun prints animal shadows from foliage
    and the artist gives shape to murmurs,
        conversations between ginkgo,

hop and dog rose. Soon her palette becomes earth
    and leaf, her sketch book,
        tree and air.

Red zeppelins of the rose hips propel above her,
    searching, searching… Dying hops
        make a doorway

from woven copper, hooked prickles on the rose
    stem beckon. All night they preserve
        a place for her.

She who sits among them by day, painting the turn
    of the year – the slow packing up and departure
        of ginkgo and dog rose

like love letters made ready for posting to the new world.

The Long Water

I lose and find myself in the long water;
I am gathered together once more

Theodore Roethke

BALLAD OF THE CLYDE'S WATER
(after Lorca and Child Ballad 216)

I: Mother's Malison

The burr of the wind whistles through the door,
pink stumps of rhubarb are breaking through the soil.
Though it is February I have the mind of autumn.
Though it is February…

The upstairs baby is crying through the wall,
the bay tree at the window wagging its branches;
huddles of leaves, the wave of a green hand.
It is February.

*

You left your imprint on the bed –
I preserve it, light a candle,
sip salt water to help my body cry.

I have visions of basking sharks,
great slow-moving shadows,
waning moons for tails –
females – come to birth in the Clyde.

I see babies in the night,
their blue-black eyes barely open,
mouths searching for their mother.

There is no hush where you are
but the endless shudder of waves,
thrum of seal and submarine,
the singing of seaweed
and algae-wrapped stone.

You will never rest, lie still, water blends
into every part of you, your heart engorged,
brain waterlogged, bones –
a creel for fish.

*

My William lies dead.
His thick hair floating on the Clyde
is a bouquet of black tulips growing
out of the river.

Who will remember you but the body that birthed you.
Who will remember you but the clouds that swallowed you.
Who will remember you but the moon you threw sticks at.
Who will remember you but your double buried under the apple.

With a torch of burning wood I light the river.
Who will remember you? Your death is forever.

*

When the time comes
I scratch your name on the back of a stone
and throw it into the Firth.

Because the river is a collector – it gathers relics from the living
        and the dead.
Because the river carries the elements out to a plastic sea.
Because the river cannot contain the warmth of your rough hands.
Because the river is a hospital corridor, swinging doors without
        end.

I have seen the rising of the Clyde, waves hurling,
thrashing the road. I have teased them as a girl,
turning as they whip my heels, rain riding my arms.

The Clyde is a dark horse permeating the mind
carrying off trees, land, the moon
and my son.

The Firth covered his face, his body sank to the maerl.
But where is he now? – The Kilbrannan Sound.
And now? – The Atlantic.

*

The house is flying around me.

I opened a window and watched him leave.
I ran a bath at the moment of his drowning.

As my body pushed him into this life
so I carried him back over the threshold.

How could I tell him not to go?
How could I tell him I saw it in a dream?

Ally bally, ally bally bee,
sittin' on yer mammy's knee

II: May Margaret

He came to the door like a flood,
the waters rising.

I was caught in the tsunami of a dream
when he came to the door;
*   my bed riding the waves.*

He came while I was sleeping
though my hair sensed he was near.

In the stranglehold of drugged sleep
     he arrived,
but I could not break free.

*

The Clyde came alive under an orchid moon
     like a thousand white snakes
and caught him by the neck.

Thundering in his ears, burning in his lungs.
                    He is searching
for a silhouette on the river bank
     but finds none.
He is searching for the blood-sun,
     break of dawn –
it does not come.

The sky withdraws like a car reversing
down a street, his arms outstretched
     like an act of supplication.

*

I came to the Gantocks to find you, William,
I followed your footsteps in my mind.
I was caught in the red eye of a beacon, William,
I was caught in a double bind.

*

The Firth and sky meet in smoky blue, light cracking the mist,
the tired body of a pier slumped in the water;
my arm burning from your last touch.

At first the Clyde came up to my ankles,
then to my knees, my chin.

Your hat caught in the wild animal
of a piece of driftwood – with tusks,
wooden tooth, wooden tongue.

Fragile ripples now roll into nothing.
I watch a gull rising in you.

You had a witch for a mother, William,
I did too.
       So now together we lie
in Clyde's water
like brother and like sister.

And we shall sleep in Clyde's water
like sister and like brother.

III: Mother's Deception

Through a closed door I spoke to him.
Through a closed door he thought I was my daughter.
Through a closed door I sent him away,
told him I had another.

           *

The arms of the rowan are split,
shooting upward,
they vibrate in the wind like a tuning fork

releasing pure tones
of sine and cosine – high pitched
like a keening mother.

For whom does she cry?
The berries are her daughters.

Plump, mushy hearts, multiplying –
there are so many of them,
each one star-kissed.

I carried a sprig with me –
bent the twigs into the shape of a cross
and sewed them into the lining of her coat.

The coat they found, like a dog
washed up on the beach,
bearing no one.

*

May Margaret, May Margaret,
why did you go?

The waves of the Clyde inhabit you.
I talk to the water, listen

to the drumming of the crab.
I dress a doll in your baby clothes,

white bonnet, mittens –
sit it on my knee.

Greetin' for a wee bawbee,
Tae buy some Coulter's candy.

THE TELEPHONE BOX

The praying mantis of an oak leaf
left in the relic of an old red telephone box

grows fat on every private conversation,
every secret flapping its wings
    against the glass.

The oak leaf lies next to the fallen
black handle of the handset as if the words,
weighing it down, were finally escaping.

I replace the handset to leave room for hope.

The shiny steel of the keypad illuminated
in the morning light is the face of someone
    who knows better.

In a dream, I blow a storm
into the mouthpiece of the handle.

Every morning I pass by the silent phone box
standing like a comedian waiting her cue.

We are both waiting for a call from across
the Holy Loch, from across the Firth of Clyde
for the voice that does not say my name.

Instead asks for the heron, the oystercatcher
    and the jackdaw.

WRITTEN ON BOARD MV CORUISK

My mind is still caught in the wind-hurled walk
down to the ferry – rain lashing my coat.
I drew it all into my body – wet knees, wet gloves,
watching the downpour whip the shining tarmac;
    black tongue of the road.

As we set sail from Dunoon, waves birl around us.
The dimmer switch of morning light gradually brightens,
small flashes of a distant shore
                break through the rain-haze.
Before long the boat shudders as we turn
into Gourock.

The waves are calmer now
and moving away from us
like concentric circles of a thrown stone.
But still I carry the gales, the rain
round inside of me as we draw into the pier;

though the waves are gentle now,
moving like a multitude of pigeons
    feeding together.

GLASGOW NIGHTS

The city falls in bursts of light around me. I am falling too.
Life in the shape of cars float across the Kingston Bridge.

Inside each car, drivers daydream. Hand on wheel,
foot on pedal, driving into the sky; faces calm as mannequins.

The bridge simply carries them. She is obedient and good.
South of the river, I walk the long road to the men and women

of swollen livers and burst hearts.
The alleyways threaten; estuaries of bin bags, middens,

rats' eyes. Souls of the Clyde float up and down,
their cold bodies offer no answers.

The air roars with the spirit of a train sliding into the glass and
        girders
of Central Station. My eyes follow the train to its destination.

The station is no home to speak of. Its rooms are museums
of the future. The Clyde river is a coming together

of the Daer and Potrail waters. And tonight
the Clyde is smooth tar; eating the light, eating the light.

HORSE LOCH
(*After Child Ballad 233*)

Prologue

I am moving beside the loch
    yet sitting still.
While rare powan breed; arctic charr, trout
and salmon swim within. The continental drift
beneath us all.

Loch Eck crackles in the morning sun… No –
Loch Eck straddles the morning sun.

Loch Eck is a woman with a corkscrew head.
Loch Eck is a double bed, covers pulled up to her neck.

Loch Eck is a couple embracing in a bath,
lichen skin thickening round them
    like blue crystals.

The late spring wind grows tough hands
on the back of the water.
The pale sky makes a girl cry,
makes another sparkle
in spite of herself.

1
Loch Eck

My hands are sleepy cats wakening into life.
Loch Eck, I peep at you between the trees.
You peep at me. Little gatherings of stones mark your shore.

Purple rhododendrons mark your shore.

I am so close to you I am sinking.
The jetty enters you the way he entered my mind unasked for.

One look, and Loch Eck, all seven miles of you
collate an image of me.
You preserve it on the bed of your drowned glen.

Today your lapping waves are a series of serene smiles.
The whitened tree branch, the glower of Beinn Mhor
welcomes me. Watching you is like watching the world's

first motion picture – Le Prince's *Roundhay Garden Scene*.
As you pass by with your jagged movements
I think of Sarah – Le Prince's mother-in-law,

dancing in her garden, 1888.
Two seconds of her turning, a solitary waltz preserved on film.
Ten days later she was dead.

2
Fairy Queen

He entered my mind like a loch.
A few seconds of his movements (like Le Prince's mother-in-law)
plays on repeat.

The way he said hello then moved sharply past me.
The way his eyes mirrored me
in a million silver halide crystals held together

by electrical attraction.
In my dreams he is a cat I'm chasing in the dark
forever keeping one step ahead of me.

I dream also of the loch, fish floating to the surface.
Their white bellies glittering mica schist.
Across the loch, hills slope like the backs of whales.

I emerge in the morning, uncurling as from a snail shell.
A dead tree is a headless snake rising up next to me.
There is a fire burning inside of me,

small flames lick my wooden body into a blaze.
My hair is smoke entrails.
I have become a strange object to myself.

I bite my lip to know that it is mine.
Loch Eck, your body is the body of a muscular horse.
In the blue hour

I stand among jetty ruins and summon
the *Fairy Queen* steamer back to your shore.

3
I, Tifty's Annie

I, Tifty's Annie, met him by fresh water.
My skin became as the leaves fluttering under the cool breeze
of his touch. Is this love?

No one can answer but every day now I see him
in stolen pieces of water between trees.
When he touched me, the loch moved inside of me.

My head floats on my body
the way the stone and tree crannog float on Loch Eck.
Police ribbon caught in the shallows speak of accidents.

Tonight, the loch has turned purple.
My body is oil spilling into the water.
My arms move among the reeds. I make waves

where logs dream and rocks sing.
The darkness at the heart of Loch Eck is the black
pumping heart muscle of a strong horse.

The crannog is an island in the air, an unlit funeral pyre,
ink blot on water. I look into the purple face
of a rhododendron. I see his face everywhere –

in the hanging valleys, the Paper Caves,
even in the slick body of a cormorant.
I come to the loch to summon his full lips, his soft hair.

4
Welcoming Spirits

I am a boulder on the shore of your narrow water.
I am visited by stones.
Black shadows make flat statues on the bottom of you.

I name him, Andrew Lammie. I conjure him by the light
of water on wet stone and twisted tree.
The mouths of reeds draw in deep breaths of lit air.

My arms ache, he is not here.
I want to gather up the loch in my skirts,
let fish encircle me. He has been sent away from me.

My father, Tifty, he beat me; my sisters scorn me.
my brother is coming for me.
I came to the loch to explore my scars.

My bruises bloom in the shape of common birds.
The chill of fresh water is in my bones.
Purple harebells ring in the hills…they ring for me.

The loch is unbreakable in the hard sunshine,
the still air. I am not unbreakable.
My brother has broken me across your rocks.

Loch Eck, I have travelled the length of you.
My last sight of you is between fragile
branches of a birch. I fold you up in my mind,

a gift to myself, and smile as the wind moves
across your quivering haunches.
I think of Le Prince's mother-in-law,

turning and turning forever on film.
Then I'm thinking of him, arriving before me
over and over. The hills are smoking,

the morning mist drifts
toward me like welcoming spirits.

AILSA CRAIG

When I catch a glimpse of her, over the hill,
the setting sun draining its pink
and red heat over her –
she is a blood moon floating on water.

    Ailsa I said
as if she were someone's mother.
I watch late clouds rest on her
until it becomes too dark to see.

    But all night she grows in my mind
like an unborn taking on new features
at every turn.
           Ailsa Craig – in daylight
her fists are blue hone granite,
her knees, common green.

All day the waves of the Clyde sail past her,
wreathes of cloud depart from her.
Nothing stays but the gannets,
the razorbills, the kittiwakes.

If I could keep her
in my pocket like a charm,
or wear her on a chain round my neck…
Ailsa Craig, in the night my mind
    returns to you.

I write your name on a slip of paper
with a question mark,
place it under my mattress.

I lie in darkness,
I wait for an answer...

AUTUMN SUNRISE

Germinating out of darkness,
a single flame birthed on the horizon.

At the edge of the Clyde
breakwater rocks take on shape and colour
suddenly like mushrooms.

My eyes are drawn to the centre of the firth, speck
of the Gantocks beacon now growing in my mind –
a dark thought that cannot align itself

with the orange heat spilling across the river,
breaking the back of the sleeping panther –
black hills of Greenock.

After death comes a sunrise,
relentlessly coming toward us with wings,
as if we were Pharaohs.

PRECIOUS STONES

Everything succumbs to the blue
and pale pink of the Arrochar Alps undulating
like a Chinese dragon on the horizon.

We are moving away from the Arrochar Alps
in a red and white ferry, crossing the Clyde Firth.
The Alps are shimmering –

dark gold and amethyst. Cirrus clouds
are a scattering of sheet music
strewn across the air.

The Arrochar Alps are faces of those I have loved
resting at peace; faces I carry with me,
like a bag of precious stones

taking them out daily, one by one,
and holding them up to the light.

REMNANT OF A PIER TEAROOM

Peeling shell, the cobby tearoom sits squatly on the pier end.
Untenanted, disused, grey finesse of the winter Clyde

colours its windows. Derelict tearoom, mired in grime,
it exists neither earth-bound nor sky. The timber cupola

of the signal tower rises, cat-like, stretching into lacklustre
steam-clouds, propping up a cast-iron weathervane

responding to signals from the salty air
thrown up from the slopes of the Clyde.

With the artistry of basking sharks, firth waves roll
in stately winter calm below the shriek of a herring gull.

The pier tearoom sails on, its ragged wings
folded, tucked in; it has nowhere else to go.

LIGHTS

Streetlights contract in the sky like jellyfish,
each with its own orbit of moonlets
and planetary dust.

It's November and the trees
on the promenade are spirits of Christmas
glitter-wrapped in white decorative lights.

The wet pavement glints beneath them.
Their reflections rise out of the ground –
two lonely figures facing each other
on the disused runway of the empty prom.

The old lights of the ferry slowly trickle
down the neck of the Clyde.

The ferry has long since departed.
It does not look back to the held out,
unshook hand of the pier.

SNOW ON THE SHINGLE

'The shore was cold with mermaids and angels.'
George Mackay Brown

We woke to a white-out; the street tippexed over
like a huge mistake corrected in a single stroke.
Yet the polished leaves of our garden shrub,
glistening jade, emerges intact untouched.

There's snow on the shingle – all the way down
    to the fringe of the Clyde.
Large pebbles and the chalk outline of a body
of seaweed protrude, occasional clumps
of seagrass' dying stalks scratch at the air.

The shore was cold with mermaids and angels.
Though we did not see them, they left footprints,
    tailprints, wingprints.
They left ice-sparkles, blizzard-breath, they left
mementos, mid-winter souvenirs of their presence.

The snow is their shed skin; it will not last.
But for now we stare into the bright gallery stretched
out before us; a gathering of light resting across

the long shingle that will soon melt then float off
into air and follow us around like gulls
    throughout the rest of the year.

SEA TANGLE

(After Child Ballad 10)

"Tangle and gold, I weave ye.
Fast to the rocks, I weave ye."
    Marjory Kennedy-Fraser

Come to the beach, sister, come
gather shellfish for dinner.
The spring sun is hotter than I remember
after so many days of cold.

      Let us sit here now, sister,
rest, lay your head on my knee
for you were up all night, wet
with the hot cries of your baby.
Rest now and I will pleat your hair
the way our mother used to.

          *

My sister brought me to the west bay
to gather limpets and petrol-blue mussels.
A clear day in March, stones
shining on the shingle
under a clean sun, a washed beach.

March – the last of winter swept away
      with the old waves.

         *

Static clouds communicate with the sun,
the sky blue as a memory.
Look ahead, see the Cowal peninsula –
the Clyde Firth dipping in and out,

curving the land. Cold blue waves
    lapping the shore.

How the beach shone before us,
pebbles like silver coins
under a glassy light;
shoreline breakers like fish
along the water's edge.
The deep blue of the Clyde.

I lift handfuls of small shells, quartz stones,
sea glass, let them run through my warm fingers.

*

I napped in the soothing sun,
head on my sister's knee.

I wake in the setting sun,
my hair tied to seaweed, bound to a rock;
the Clyde is coming for me.
The distant ghost hills are snow-shaped,
the Clyde is coming for me.

Darkening water is moving in, spume scattered.
Dormant waves suddenly draw near, moon-shunted.
Moon particles burn on the Clyde's back.

I am stuck – rocks behind, water in front.
I am trying to become a fish, grow gills and swim
to my baby. My breasts leak milk into seaweed.
I am part-shore now, part-water.

The Gantocks beacon swings its light past me.
Highland Mary is looking down on me
holding her bronze skirts

on a hill of flowering gorse, dull
in dusky light.

Clyde come quickly, don't dillydally at my feet.
I welcome you into my mouth,
lift my hair, my weightless body.
I have given up on my child now
as I let go of the mussel shells in my hands,
blue embryos.

Out of the water I came,
to water I go.

Mother Moon

The moon's my mother: how I love the moon!

Theodore Roethke

IGLOO

The Cheshire cat smiles of our son,
our daughter crouched in a snow-den
    in the heart of the garden.

In the igloo they could be anywhere –
riding the thorax of a cabbage white butterfly
or under the wing of a white goose.

Our children huddle inside the dome of the igloo,
built by your bare hands –
our very own tomb of Agamemnon.

The sun is a dim torchlight
    behind clouds.
I welcome the heavy snows, Siberian wind.
I welcome this memorable white spell

to wipe away the last harsh winter of my mother –
the crisp Antartica
            of the high dependency unit
where she spent her final hours.

Like an igloo, her small room
was pristine clean, oxygen tank
    funnelling pure air
into her inflated lungs. I breathe in
the burn of the snow air.

Our children could be anywhere –
wrapped in the tight bud of a white rose;
harnessed to a snow moon;
or with my mother, in the hospital bed,
their smiles – a warm star
on either side of her.

HER HAIR IS A LANDSCAPE OF ITS OWN
for Ruby

I am scaling the cliff face of her hair to reach her –
my summit-daughter, hair-raiser, my blood-
stone girl. She is a cut asterism adorning an armour
of hair. When I loosen her pleats, a storm rises.
February gales batter our windows, Clyde squalls
tie ships to their harbours. The cinnamon falls
of her hair engulf me, follow me like notes
plucked from a guitar – each string vibrating
through the air, music from a girl's hair.

The girl is my ten-year-old daughter.
Daily I traverse her jungle, Medusa snakes
squirming between us. Growing for so long,
brushed, combed, the hair of my daughter
is her signature. The hair of my daughter
wraps her up in a hair parcel – all bows
and ribbons with the bark of a feral dog.
The hair of my daughter is her doppelganger –
her image is caught in its many folds.

It knows the language of pony tails, braids,
bands and bobbles. Her hair has been dyed red,
dyed purple. Her hair hangs around her,
coiling when it senses danger.
My daughter's hair is as old as the Hanging
Gardens of Babylon, mysterious as the riddle
of the Sphinx and the riddle grows day by day.

MARCH SNOW

for Sorley & Andrew

The road is foreign – the ground hidden,
walls have grown white heads, snow bodies
not children play on the swings.

In the car park, cars are mounds
hunched next to each other
    like armadillos.

A boy in yellow and a boy in blue,
each of them armed with a shovel. They do a snow dance
on the driveway – scooping up soft inches

and flinging them into the garden. The snow
itself follows its own choreography – fluttering
through the air like a kaleidoscope

of cabbage white butterflies,
oblivious to the coming rain.

MARCH MOONESS

March moon ducks behind fast flowing spume-clouds
pouring across the sky, wind-whipped and pinkish mauve
against the navy night, against the moon-bulb flowering
between cloud-blast, March mooness. The sky is no respite
for the eye, for the mind. It is a swift passing. Clouds
are unbuttoned shirts flapping round me, drawing me
into a promise of warmth, of arms, of heldness.
Will the clouds hold? Will March moon come out?
Will the night air envelop me? I envelop the night air.

METAPHORS FOR A DAYLIGHT MOON

Moon is skin of cloud, tusk of pig,
tooth and nail, perfect smile.

Moon is edge of pearl, sky tiara,
bushy eyebrow, pram wheel.

Moon is daisy petal, glass ceiling,
wing of swan, satin bow.

Moon is sklif of bone, hem of skirt,
broken shell, wave spume.

Moon is cigarette smoke, lock of hair,
curve of calf, lotus foot.

Moon is spilled semen, baby's heel,
sunken dinghy, fish tail.

Moon is broken saucer, bomb crater,
calcium rock, this white page.

Moon is platinum band, gull feather,
hem of dress, bra strap.

Moon is grave votive, fairy light,
hull of sub, spirit level.

Moon is quilt corner, playground swing,
crook of arm, wind turbine.

Moon is arc of missile, crust of ice,
doctor's pill, this last breath.

COBWEB

A dandelion seed mimics
    a small fly
caught in the mathematical guy ropes
stretched between fence panels
like chewing gum.

Stretched as far as they can travel,
perhaps as far back
    as childhood
from one mouth to another.

The setting sun lights up the web
as it tattoos the air
between panels of a green fence.

The cobweb is a cat's cradle
to catch the western sun as she slides
out from between the sheets
      of the sky.

This web is no place to die.
It is a birth caul.

Like a cracked mirror, the web
spills its breakages from the centre.

To look into a spider web
is to see the mechanics of the world:
corridors of space and light
      (whatever these things are).

I eat the silk of the web to strengthen me
        for the coming days;
its rays fortify my heart.

The cobweb is there and it is not there.
Like the strangeness of domesticity
in the early days of grief.

REST AND BE THANKFUL

for Jamie

On the *Rest* we lie
back on tarmac eyeing up
the winter sky: Pleiades, Plough, Orion.
Drive. The Milky Way suspends
above the hollow glen, high
high up the Drover's Road. Bend
into its curves, *take no thought for the morrow*
just drive. The highway kneels before us
and the windscreen is riddled with galaxies
strewn across the rotunda night.
Tonight, there is no loch, no Firth of Clyde
smack into a beach wall, only a pumpkin moon
and the Glasgow road carved from a mountainside.

CHRISTMAS CANDLES

On the red tablecloth, four candles – two tall in fluted bronze,
two in the cut-out mouths of glass stars. Four teardrop flames
      bless my table.

The eye of a buzzard overlooks them. Open palms of the
      poinsettia
beg on the windowsill. In the quiet hour, the red and white
      candles

are in command. Upright, they are herons. Motionless in the
      shallows
of my table waiting, waiting. In the quiet hour, my heart knocks

against my chest and the white candles flicker, collared saints.
They watch over me, their heads – flaming halos. Their halos
      radiating

moon rings – the cirrus clouds of my mother and her
      mother, all the mothers
before me in this moment summoned by the high-altitude
      particles

that visit me now, this late Christmas evening in the middle
      years
of my life. The candles are given up to light and heat. Bronze
      wrists

grip the red candles, a tiny ball of wax drips down the red body.
Leather-backed dining chairs are tucked into the table

like pigs at a trough. Two hares hold up a lamp. Marble etchings
of a gloomy landscape – grey boulders, silhouette of a single pine

tree, on the wall. *I am the red candle. I am the white.*
Though we stand side by side on the table, we shall never touch

in this life. Our cirrus clouds mingle in the air. In the quiet hour,
when last drinks drain from small glasses, the tv falls asleep and
            mobile

phones, like tired out puppies, gently snore on the bedside
            table. Rituals
of every household up and down the street – switch off the lights,

lock the doors to lie down in darkness like a blown-out candle,
            alone
and waiting for sunrise to knock at the window, send messages
            on the phone.

NOTES

'The Brahan Seer's Wife'

The Brahan Seer, Kenneth Mackenzie (known in Gaelic as Coinneach Odhar), was a 17th century Highland prophet whose prophesies are said to have foretold a wide range of events from the Battle of Culloden to WW2.

'Ballad of the Clyde's Water'

"Ally Bally Bee" also known as "Coulter's Candy" is a traditional Scots folk song written by Robert Coltart.

'Horse Loch'

The Roundhay Garden Scene is a short film (less than 3 seconds long) shot by French inventor Louis Le Prince in 1888. It is thought to be the first celluloid motion picture ever made.

'Rest and Be Thankful'

Rest and Be Thankful is the name given to a section of the A83 at the top of Glen Croe reflecting the long, steep climb of the road. The words were inscribed on a stone by soldiers in the 1750's on completion of the original military road after the Jacobite uprisings.